[CODING YOUR PASSION™]

USING COMPUTER SCIENCE IN AUTOMOTIVE CAREERS

JENNIFER CULP

Rosen YA™
New York

Published in 2019 by The Rosen Publishing Group, Inc.
29 East 21st Street, New York, NY 10010

First Edition

Library of Congress Cataloging-in-Publication Data

Names: Culp, Jennifer, 1985– author.
Title: Using computer science in automotive careers / Jennifer Culp.
Description: New York : Rosen Publishing, 2019. | Series: Coding your passion | Includes bibliographical references and index. | Audience: Grades 7–12.
Identifiers: LCCN 2018010900| ISBN 9781508183884 (library bound) | ISBN 9781508183877 (pbk.)
Subjects: LCSH: Automotive computers—Vocational guidance—Juvenile literature. | Automobiles—Software—Vocational guidance—Juvenile literature. | Automobiles—Electronic equipment—Vocational guidance—Juvenile literature. | Computer programming—Vocational guidance—Juvenile literature. | Automobile industry and trade—Vocational guidance—Juvenile literature.

Classification: LCC TL272.53 .C85 2019 | DDC 629.2/72023—dc23
LC record available at https://lccn.loc.gov/2018010900

Manufactured in the United States of America

CONTENTS

INTRODUCTION

What exactly is a computer? At its essence, a computer is a machine that performs arithmetic based on patterns of fluctuating electrical voltage. This machine interprets voltage into a series of "on" and "off" signals and performs actions in response to this input. Machine code, a language that computers can understand directly, can be used to communicate commands to the computer. Then, the commands may be combined into processes, which tell the machine how to perform increasingly sophisticated actions. As processes combine and interact, computers can carry out seriously complicated actions.

So, machine code—that's how computers think, but it's an awfully inconvenient method of communication for human beings who want to interact with computers. That's where programming languages come in. A program, or a set of instructions that tells a computer how to perform complex tasks, encompasses a lot of machine code. Rather than write out the entire program in a seemingly endless sequence of ones and zeros, a programmer instead uses a programming language to write the code (which will subsequently be translated back into source code the computer can understand and carry out). There are thousands of programming languages, and they all allow human "coders" to write instructions for computers.

Computers in cars go far beyond the electronics you use to listen to music and monitor the road. Without computers, a modern car can't run at all.

That's fascinating, sure, but what does it have to do with your car? Well, here's the thing: there are computers in your car. And not just the ones that operate the navigation or electronic lock systems, either: computers are responsible for controlling the very mechanisms that make modern cars stop and go. "It would be easy to say the modern car is a computer on wheels, but it's more like 30 or more computers on wheels," said Bruce Emaus, chair of SAE International's embedded software standards committee, in a *New York Times* article. These electronic control units (ECUs) control systems such as braking, ignition, suspension, cruise control, entertainment systems, climate control, and odometers in personal vehicles. "The electronic systems in modern cars and trucks," wrote Jim Motavalli in the same *New York Times* article, "are packed with up to 100 million lines of computer code, more than in some jet fighters."

Without computers, cars don't start, don't run, don't brake, and definitely don't play songs on the radio. Without code, cars don't function. Anyone who's interested in understanding how cars really work needs an understanding of that code—including car designers, car mechanics, and even car app developers.

CHAPTER ONE

A CAR OR A COMPUTER?

Computers were first incorporated into car design in the late 1970s. According to the *New York Times*, the Oldsmobile Toronado included a simple computer unit to control spark plug timing as early as 1977, followed by an optional trip computer in the 1978 Cadillac Seville. However, the real driving force behind the adoption of ECUs was the call for emissions regulation beginning in the 1970s. ECUs helped handle functions such as ignition timing and transmission shifting, helping conserve fuel and reduce unnecessary pollution.

In the 1980s, computer-managed engine systems allowed for computer-controlled electronic fuel injection. ECUs facilitated the development of safety features, such as antilock brakes and skid control. Today, many cars are equipped with computer-automated automatic braking features, blind-spot cameras, and even "smart" speed-regulating cruise control. Today, a car may contain anywhere from thirty to fifty networked and/or independent central processing units (CPUs), which control everything from the car's suspension system to the back seat passenger television screen. In the future, the level of sophistication is expected to continue rising: "Cars have taken over from jets in terms of advancements and carrying forward technology," said Ross McKenzie, managing director of the University of Waterloo's Centre for Automotive Research, in an article for the *Globe and Mail*.

IMPROVING EFFICIENCY WITH COMPUTERS

The system of wires and software protocols that acts as connective tissue between a vehicle's computers and sensors is called a CANbus, or CAN for short, which stands for controller area network. CAN allows cars to be made more cheaply and efficiently and provides them with capabilities that wouldn't have been possible before its invention.

CAN functions like a freeway system for the data collected by a car's computers. ECUs act like traffic lights and intersections for the data moving through the system. Each ECU has multiple jobs, like locking and unlocking the doors, rolling windows up and down, or controlling the engine and transmission. Each ECU has sensors and switches wired in to provide it with information such as the temperature, pressure, voltage, acceleration, braking, steering angle, position of the vehicle, and more.

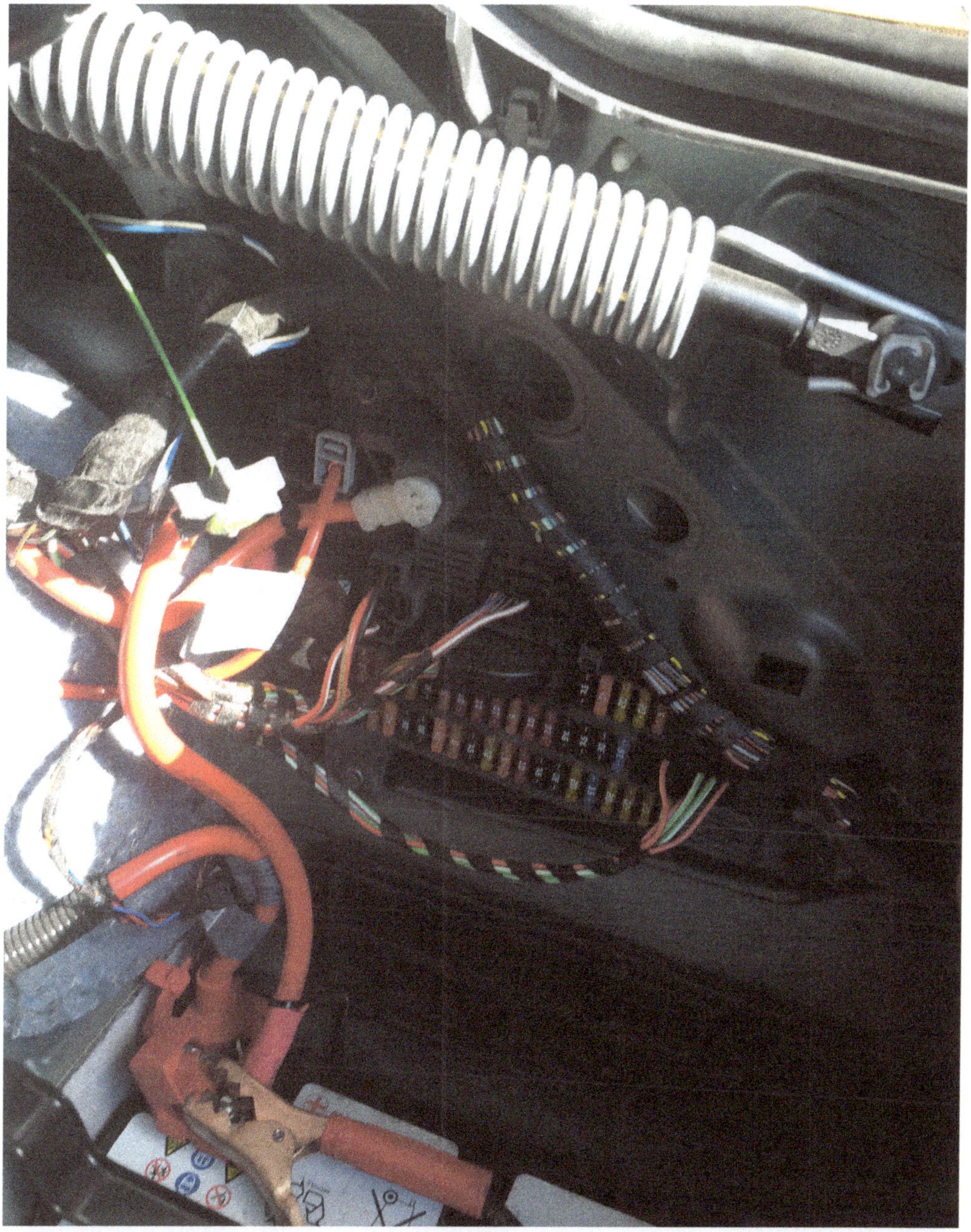

The CANbus dramatically reduced the amount of wiring necessary to make modern cars functional. This simple-looking system allows a lot of information to flow constantly throughout the running vehicle.

That's what CAN facilitates. The CANbus allows data to move through the "freeway" between ECUs constantly: each computer reports its sensor and programming information constantly. As this data freely circulates through the system, each individual ECU "listens" to catch information relevant to its assigned duties. There is no central hub or routing system but instead a continuous flow of information that is constantly available to all of the ECUs.

This constant stream of data is what allows for engineering feats such as electronically controlled sliding doors in minivans. When the ECU that controls the door gets the signal to close, for example, it doesn't just automatically close the door. First, it checks the data stream to make sure the van is parked before carrying out the command. Then, the ECU continues to monitor for a voltage spike in the door's motors, which might be caused by an arm or object in the door's path. If so, the ECU reverses the direction of the door for safety. If nothing gets in the way and the door closes successfully, the ECU automatically locks it.

This sequence of actions is made possible by the minivan's CANbus. Before CAN, merely electrically powering the door would require dedicated wires running between the van's shifter, door switch, and motor. Before CAN, convenient features like electronically powered door locks and windows meant miles and miles of wire in thick bundles snaked all throughout a car's inner mechanisms. With CAN, a door lock button and the lock mechanism don't have to be directly wired together; instead, they can "talk" to one another over the existing CAN network. However, just because CAN simplified physical engineering in cars doesn't mean that it's necessarily less complex—now the burden of networking and coordinating each of the car's devices falls on programming.

However, the simplification of a car's wiring harness wasn't the driving force behind the implementation of CAN. In the 1970s, California led the world in pushing for vehicle emissions control to prevent pollution. This effort led to the development of the on-board diagnostics (OBD) protocol, which requires a CAN network for the vehicle to effectively perform a self-diagnosis. This means that a designated ECU can watch the network for problem reports, which are broadcast as OBD-II codes. If the ECU detects an OBD-II problem code, it turns the Check Engine light on. A mechanic can then determine what the problem is merely by checking the code. Whenever modern cars are turned on, they constantly use the stream of data flowing through the CAN network to perform these self-diagnostic checks.

Not only can mechanics make use of the CAN network to check on errors that set off a warning light; even private car owners can do it. Standard cars have a data port easily accessible to the driver, usually below the steering column. Anyone who plugs a handheld code reader into this port receives a fault code, which can then be investigated on the internet or interpreted by an automotive technician. If the problem is physical, a mechanic may be needed to fix it. But sometimes errors exist in the software rather than the physical elements of the vehicle. If a computer glitch is discovered or the car manufacturer wishes to make an upgrade to the car's software, a technician uses the same data port to plug in a computer and simply upload a new algorithm. Before the implementation of CAN, a mechanic would have to physically replace an ECU to perform a software modification.

In the past five years, aftermarket equipment has been developed that allows drivers to check their own OBD-II connection to get useful statistics such as instant fuel economy, engine speed, temperature, and vehicle speed. Combined with smartphone apps for acceleration and Global Positioning System (GPS), this information can provide a sophisticated view of a car's performance and efficiency.

In fact, the CAN network and data port make it possible for tinkerers to hack

When the engine malfunction light comes on, that's an ECU letting you know there's a problem somewhere within the system.

a car to bypass manufacturer specifications and make changes such as increasing the top speed. Manufacturers disapprove of this practice and void warranties for hacked vehicles. It's inadvisable to experiment with hacking a car unless you're armed with a computer science degree—as Ben Wojdyla warned in *Popular Mechanics*, a mistake could leave you with "a car-shaped driveway ornament" rather than a functioning vehicle. However, if you're a car-specific embedded software engineer or software-experienced mechanic, tinkering with a vehicle's programming is your job! Eventually, dealer visits for software upgrades could even be replaced by an at-home cellular-connected cloud download. However, that's still far off in the future.

THE COST OF CODE

In a 1983 article in *IEEE Transactions on Industrial Electronics*, GM engineer Jonas Bereisa predicted that "software development will become the single most important consideration in new product development engineering." Today, it is estimated that more than 80 percent of automobile innovations come from computer code, and software has become the major contributor of price in new cars.

As a percentage of vehicle cost, software climbed from 5 percent in the late 1970s to around 15 percent by 2005, and in hybrid cars, where

the amount of software needed is about twice as much as that of a traditional car, the cost of electronics as a percent of vehicle costs is closer to 45 percent. In the next couple of years, some experts predict that electronic costs will rise to about 50 percent for traditional vehicles and 80 percent for hybrids.

Manfred Broy, a professor of informatics at Technical University in Munich, Germany, estimates that if it costs about $10 per line of developed code in a premium car, the vehicle's software alone represents nearly one billion dollars worth of investment.

Complexity comes at a cost. According to IBM, about 50 percent of car warranty costs were related to electronics and embedded software as of 2009. In 2005, Toyota recalled 160,000 2004 and early model 2005 Prius hybrids because of a software problem that caused the car to suddenly stall or shut down. At 90 minutes of repair time per vehicle to fix the faulty software—about 240,000 total hours of labor—the voluntary recall proved quite expensive for the company.

Chrysler, Volkswagen, and GM performed similar recalls in 2008 in order to fix software problems related to automotive transmission, air conditioning, and air bags to ensure driver and passenger safety. As IEEE Spectrum writer Robert Charette pointed out in 2009, it is a tribute to automotive software developers that there aren't many more recalls given all the software in cars.

HOW "CAN" CAME TO BE

The CAN serial bus system was first introduced by Bosch GmbH, an engineering and electronics company, at the Society of Automotive Engineers (SAE) congress in February 1986. Today, almost every car manufactured contains at least one CAN network. CAN is also used in other types of vehicles, like trains and ships, and even in industrial controls, and it is probably the leading serial bus system worldwide.

CAN was first dreamed up in the early 1980s, when engineers for Bosch began evaluating the serial bus systems available at the time to potentially adapt them for use in

CAN isn't just used in personal passenger cars. It's also used in other vehicles such as trains and ships.

passenger cars. A vehicle bus system is the vehicle's specialized internal communications network, which connects the various components of the vehicle and allows them to "talk" to one another. None of the existing bus systems in the early 1980s was suitable for the needs of automotive engineers, so in 1983 a man named Uwe Kiencke began developing a new one. The system would go on to reduce the miles of wire in existing wiring harnesses and also add new functionalities to the automobiles in which it would be equipped.

The new bus system was a collaborative effort that included engineers from Mercedes-Benz and Intel. A consulting professor from the University of Applied Sciences in Braunschweig-Wolfenbüttel, Germany, named the network protocol CAN, the name by which the world would eventually come to know it.

CAN was officially introduced in February 1986 at the SAE congress in Detroit, Michigan, where it was called the Automotive Serial Controller Area Network. With no central bus master, the new multimaster network protocol was based on a mechanism to grant the bus access to the highest-priority message without delay. Additionally, the new bus included several error-detection mechanisms, which allowed for automatic disconnection of faulty bus nodes so that functional nodes could continue to communicate without interruption.

The primary difference between the new system and old buses was innovative: now the transmitted messages were identified by their content, rather than the node address of the transmitter or receiver of the message. Furthermore, the identifier representing the

FIXING CODE-DRIVEN CARS

There are no federal educational or certification requirements in place to become a working automotive mechanic. Due to legal reasons, though, most employers require that anyone seeking to become a mechanic be at least eighteen years of age. Additionally, most employers prefer that their mechanics hold either a high school diploma or a general equivalency diploma, which is also a requirement to earn an associate's degree or attend a vocational training program. Furthermore, high school education provides aspiring mechanics with a solid math and science background to understand complex subjects, such as engine controls, fuel injection systems, and, of course, code. Some community colleges or vocational schools may even allow students to enter an automotive program while they are still working to obtain a high school or general equivalency diploma. Traditional college programs that lead to a bachelor's degree last four years. Most college-based automotive programs offer associate's degrees, which may be completed in two years. Technical and trade schools may also offer shorter sessions that provide particular specialty certificates in a matter of weeks. As in most occupations, more education tends to provide more career opportunity and higher paychecks.

content of the message was able to specify the priority of the message within the system.

CAN became a reality in 1987 when computer chip company Intel delivered the first CAN control chip, the 82526, followed shortly by the Philips Semiconductors 82C200. These two "earliest ancestors of CAN controllers," as the CAN in Automation (CiA) website refers to them, were different: the 82526 "FullCAN" concept required less CPU load than the 82C200 but was limited in the number of messages it could receive. The 82C200 "BasicCAN" required less silicon.

Today, CAN can even let your car radio link up with your phone for convenient control. CarPlay enables a car radio to be a display and controller for an iPhone.

Today, the terms "FullCAN" and "BasicCAN" have become obsolete, as succeeding CAN chips have implemented a mixture of both concepts. The first CAN international standard was published in 1993.

Although CAN was developed for use in passenger cars, it became very popular with a variety of other applications. In Finland, an elevator manufacturer called Kone used the CANbus in its products. Textile machine manufacturers Lindauer Dornier and Sulzer founded the CAN Textile User's Group. In the Netherlands, Philips Medical Systems used CAN for internal communication in X-ray machines. Each of these different applications offered the opportunity for new research and development of the technology. In 1992, the CiA group was founded to promote the technical enhancement of CAN and market its use in various applications. Today, most passenger vehicles incorporate multiple CAN networks to connect all the components of the vehicle.

CHAPTER TWO

CARS AND CODE

Mechanics use code to determine exactly what is wrong with a vehicle so that they can fix it. All vehicles produced since 1996 are required to be compliant with the OBD system, OBD II. OBD-II parameter identifications (PIDs) are used by mechanics to figure out what systems specifically require repair. How does it work? OBD-II–compliant vehicles are all equipped with a connector, which must be located within 3 feet (.91 meters) of the driver (usually beneath the steering column). An auto technician plugs a scan tool into the connector to find the diagnostic trouble code affecting the vehicle. The scan tool sends a PID signal to the car's CANbus. The CANbus recognizes which device is responsible for the PID and reports its value to the computer, which then sends a response to the scan tool for the technician to read and determine what is wrong with the vehicle.

A laptop is one of a modern mechanic's most important tools, letting her know exactly what's wrong with a specific component of the vehicle so she can fix it properly.

The history of OBD begins in the late 1960s, around the time computer chips were first being introduced into cars. Development was driven by environmental protection agencies concerned about limiting emissions, including the California Air Resources Board, the SAE, the International Organization for Standardization, and the US Environmental Protection Agency, according to senior embedded systems engineer Victor Barreto, who wrote a history of OBD systems for the Geotab website with Daniela Mooers.

Car manufacturer Volkswagen introduced the very first OBD computer system with scanning capability in 1968. A decade later, Datsun released its own OBD system with limited, nonstandardized ability. In 1980, General Motors (GM) created a proprietary scannable interface capable of providing engine diagnostics, like many other manufacturers at the time.

Before the advent of standardization, each manufacturer created its own specific system. Every tool from a different manufacturer had its own connector type, electronic interface requirements, and custom problem codes. This lack of standardization was confusing and couldn't continue forever.

In 1988, the SAE called for a standard connector and set of diagnostics. In 1991, OBD I was introduced when the state of California required all cars sold in the state to have some form of basic OBD. In 1994, California went further to mandate that all vehicles sold in the state starting in 1996 have OBD as

An OBD port is the key to understanding what's going on within a car's computer system. With this tool, mechanics determine what's wrong with any malfunctioning part of a vehicle.

recommended by the SAE, now called OBD II. In 1996, the rest of the United States followed suit, enforcing mandatory OBD II for all vehicles manufactured or sold within the country.

Through OBD II, mechanics can access status information and diagnostic trouble codes for the power train (engine and transmission) and emissions control systems, as well as access the vehicle identification number, calibration identification number, ignition

ASE ACES

Certification with the National Institute for Automotive Service Excellence, known as the ASE, demonstrates mastery in the field and makes a mechanic or automotive technician a competitive job applicant. ASE certification examinations are offered in a number of different specialties and are undertaken once a mechanic has worked professionally for a period of at least two years to secure suitable experience prior to becoming certified.

The ASE, founded in 1972, is a nonprofit organization that serves to standardize and improve the quality of vehicle repair and service. ASE certification benefits automotive technicians, who can use it to provide proof of their technical knowledge, and also shop owners and service customers, who have assurance of a technician's level of expertise before contracting his or her services.

counter, and emissions control system counters. Numerous trouble codes cover various areas of the vehicle, including the power train, body, chassis, and network. Now when a car is taken to a mechanic for service, he or she can just connect a scanning tool to the OBD port in order to receive the trouble codes and identify the problem. This convenience allows mechanics to inspect cars much more quickly and accurately diagnose malfunctions before they become major problems.

And that's not all OBD II accomplishes. OBD II also allows GPS fleet tracking devices to collect information on variables such as fuel usage, fault codes, vehicle speed, and engine revolutions. When uploaded to a software interface, this information allows fleet managers to monitor trip start and finish times, overrevving, speeding, excessive idling, fuel consumption, and more, providing a complete picture of vehicle use and performance.

CHIPS CHIPS CHIPS

"The car of the future will be the most powerful computer you will ever own, packing the processing power of a supercomputer into a box the size of a car stereo," a representative for American chip maker Nvidia told Sophie Curtis in an article for the *Telegraph*. Nvidia started out making computer chips for video game consoles and laptop computers but starting in the early 2000s, it began adapting chips for use in cars. In 2009, the third-generation Audi

The introduction of self-driving cars could help blind or elderly drivers who are not able to safely operate a traditional vehicle become more independent.

V8 became the first car to use an Nvidia graphics processor in its 3D navigation system. Now Nvidia has graphics chips in more than eight million cars on the road, including models made by Tesla, Honda, Volkswagen, and Mercedes-Benz. The company intends to continue working to improve the quality of car-specific chips. "Younger first-time car buyers have grown up with iPhones and iPads, so the expectation is that if you're going to spend this much money on a car, the electronics in the car should be at least as good as your tablet," said Dan Shapiro, senior director of automotive at Nvidia. Shapiro said that the company aspires to make future cars' navigation screens better integrated into each vehicle while providing a detailed view of the world outside.

The 2015 Tegra X1 processor that powered Nvidia's then-cutting-edge Drive CX cockpit visualization computer delivered the same amount of power as a 1,600-square-foot (149-square-meter) supercomputer in the year 2000, displaying textures such as carbon fiber, brushed metal, and glass in a photorealistic fashion. Advanced lighting effects allow it to render 3D maps and landmarks, and it can also provide detailed surround vision to help with parking and maneuvering.

Though Nvidia in 2015 was only what Curtis described as a "niche player" in an automotive chip industry dominated by companies such as Texas Instruments, Intel, and Qualcomm, the company had already booked more than $2 billion in future automotive business by 2015. This is likely due in part to Nvidia's ambition to lead the driverless car market. The company debuted its Drive PX autopilot computer in 2015, which uses twelve high-definition cameras and patented deep learning that identifies objects surrounding the car and determines how to navigate safely.

Developers help the computer "learn" by feeding it information in advance, so it adapts to be able to recognize all types of road signs, different lanes, other cars, and pedestrians when it functions in real time. If the car encounters something in real life that it didn't encounter in the model uploaded to its computers in the data center, it sends the information back to the cloud so it can be included in the next training set and make the car grow successively "smarter."

Nvidia worked with Audi on zFAS autonomous driving technology, demonstrated at the January 2015 Consumer Electronics Show in Las Vegas when a prototype driverless Audi A7 piloted itself 550 miles (885 kilometers) from San Francisco to arrive at the event. Though test self-driving vehicles at Google have been involved in accidents, proponents of driverless vehicles insist that autonomous cars will eventually serve to reduce accidents caused by human error.

Many people prefer to drive, and experts predict that the future will bring computer-aided driving, which will allow the driver to put the car into auto-driving mode or choose to drive himself or herself. However, if automated driving systems prove to dramatically reduce incidents of accidents, injuries, and fatalities, computer-controlled cars could eventually become mandatory.

HOW CARS LEARN

In January 2017, Cars.com writer Nick Kurczewski went for a ride in a self-piloted deep-learning Audi at

WHY CODE?

"Software is becoming a critical layer of all our lives. It is the language of our world. In the future, not knowing the language of computers will be as challenging as being illiterate or innumerate are today," wrote Dan Crow in an article for the *Guardian*. Computational thinking, combining math, logic, and algorithms, is a boon for any automotive technician. Computational thinking breaks large problems down into smaller ones, making them more manageable to tackle. Focusing on the most pertinent aspects of a problem allows complex problems to be solved in efficient ways and builds specific solutions into general answers. Most importantly, computational thinking not only helps people design cars but also helps people figure out how to fix them.

the Consumer Electronics Show in Las Vegas. The deep-learning capability allows for prototype computer-driven cars to adapt and respond appropriately to unfamiliar environments.

As Kurczewski explained, the Audi Q7 SUV in which he rode didn't come equipped with extra cameras or elaborate sensors, relying solely on Nvidia's Drive PX deep-learning platform to operate safely. The Nvidia Drive PX platform uses camera-enabled surround vision, sensor fusion, and computer deep learning to pilot a car safely around and through obstacles on the road. "It is capable of understanding in real-time what's happening around the vehicle, precisely locating itself on an HD map, and planning a safe path forward," says the company's website. Over one thousand times more powerful than a home computer, the PX chip can support the feeds of up to twelve high-resolution cameras and process 1.3 gigapixels of information every second.

Kurczewski was impressed with the results: "The pared-back nature of the autonomous Audi shows how far this tech can go on its own, and how AI [artificial intelligence] could speed up the arrival of self-driving cars," he wrote. Kurczewski's test ride around a track featuring curves, corners, loose gravel, and a construction barrier went smoothly, "though some

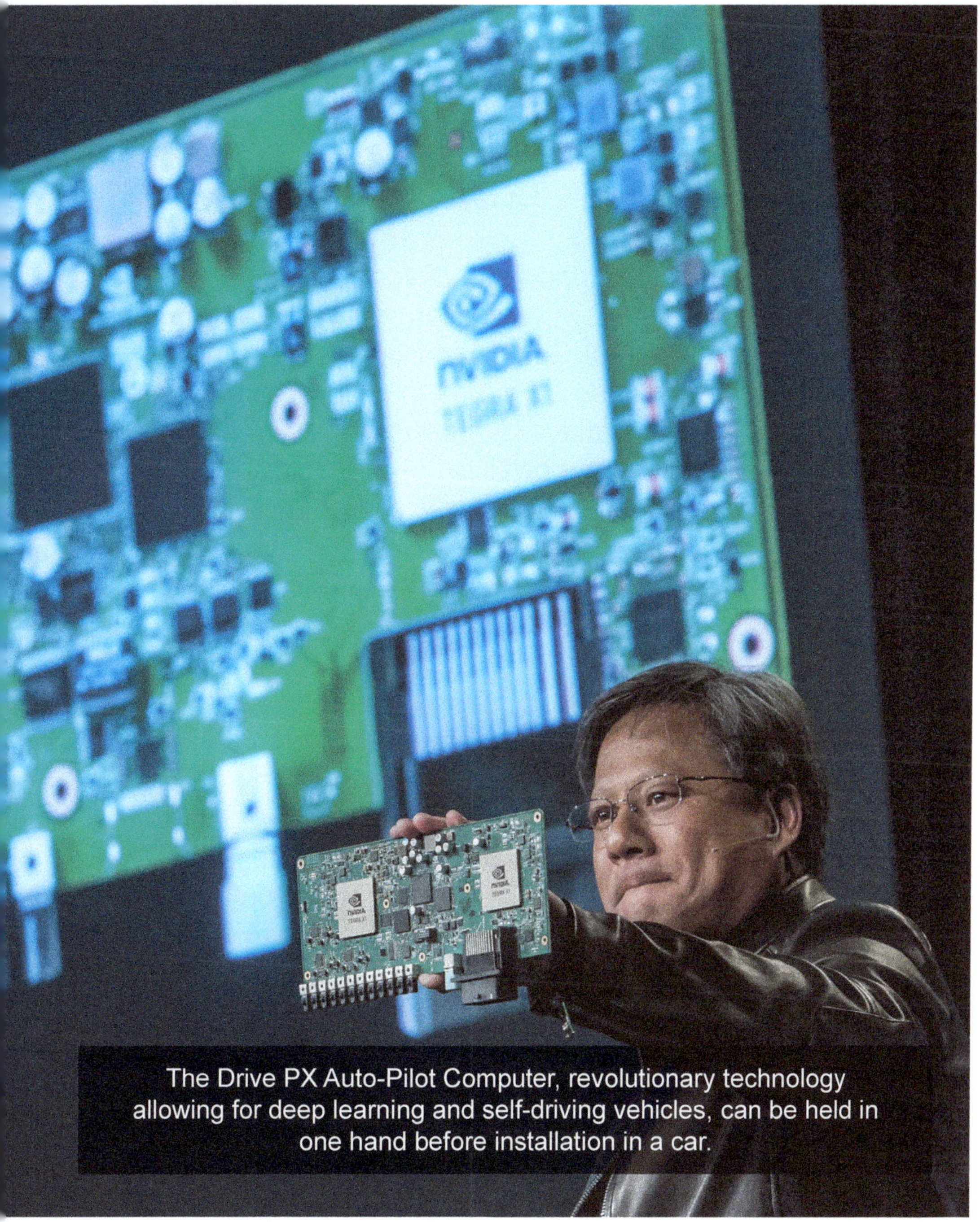

The Drive PX Auto-Pilot Computer, revolutionary technology allowing for deep learning and self-driving vehicles, can be held in one hand before installation in a car.

of the steering inputs seemed overly complicated for the turns involved," he noted. The ride was a success. However, only hours earlier another Nvidia vehicle, a Lincoln MKZ sedan, was forced to slam on its brakes to stop itself from running off the course. Vehicular deep learning is advancing rapidly, but it still has some problems to overcome.

To create fully autonomous driverless cars, engineers must perfect tech in at least eleven areas, according to an article in *Car and Driver* magazine: lidar, ultrasonic sensors, radar, high-definition mapping, cameras, backup brake actuators, tire monitors, V2X communications, power supply, "brains," and information autobahn. Lidar (light detection and ranging) sensors, which can send out five-nanosecond bursts of laser, which then bounce back to the sensors, will be needed to map objects up to 300 yards (274 m) away, even in the dark. Ultrasonic sensors will be needed to map surroundings at low speeds, and radar must be better adapted to a car's shape to provide a wider field of view.

To accurately pinpoint a car in its environment, the information from lidar, ultrasonic sensors, and radar must be cross-referenced with a high-definition map stored aboard the vehicle. Cameras, which are already in use on many current-model cars, can be used to coordinate 360-degree surround-view parking. The key to safety in computer-controlled vehicles is redundancy: making sure there are multiple backups to maintain all functions in case any one system fails.

An electronically controlled actuator capable of applying pressure to the hydraulic system to slow

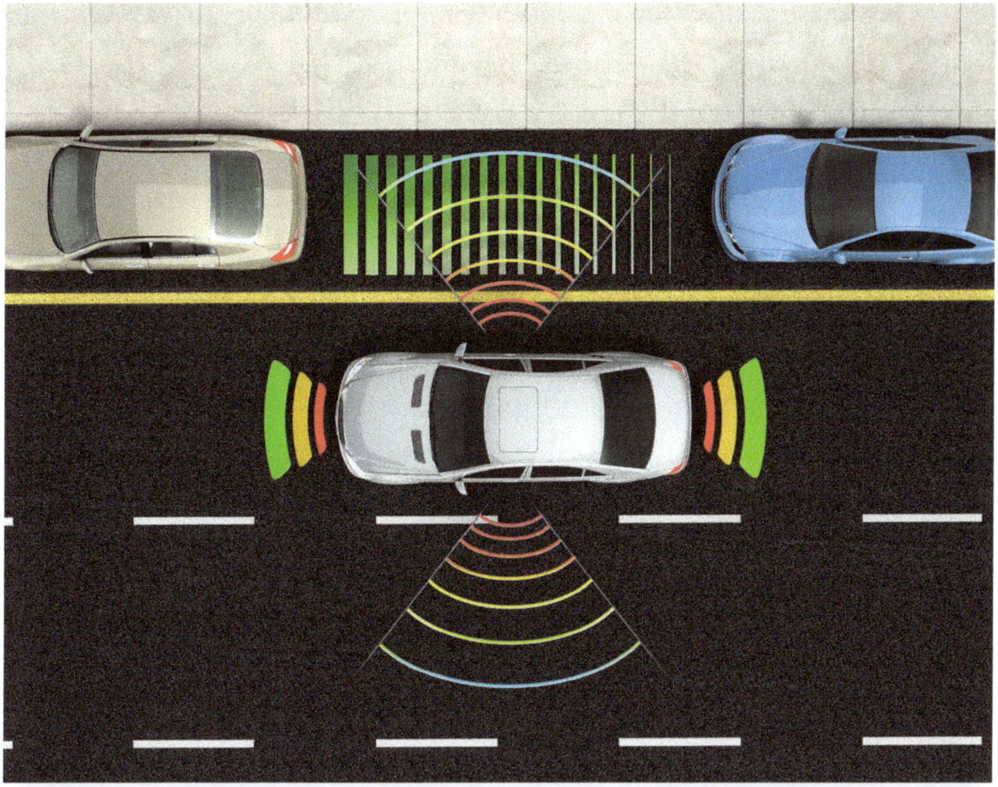

In smart cars being developed today, high-resolution cameras assist with functions such as parking and avoiding obstacles on the road.

the vehicle in the case of brake failure will be vital to the success of any computer-piloted passenger vehicle. Tire monitors can provide the computer with information that lets it know how to maintain following distance to allow for sufficient room for emergency braking.

Connection to cellular networks, or V2X, will be required to transmit data between the car and cloud storage, while dedicated short-range radio frequencies can carry information from vehicle to vehicle (V2V) or vehicle to a pedestrian's devices (V2P).

Batteries will be necessary to guard against electrical failure—and as for the brains? A platform such as Continental Automotive's Assisted & Automated Drive Control Unit translates data streams into a digital re-creation of the car's environment. With this capability, the control unit can determine a safe course of travel and communicate the path of travel to the vehicle's drive, steering, and braking systems.

And finally, information autobahn involves Category 5 Ethernet cables that will transmit data from the sensors to the drive control unit.

CHAPTER THREE

PROGRAMMING VEHICLES

Computer hardware describes the physical components that make up a computer. Computer software is the various collections of code installed onto the computer's hardware. In a device such as an automobile, the CANbus, the "brains" of the car, is a nontraditional type of hardware. The car itself essentially functions as hardware, while the code that tells it how to perform actions is software.

People who write code for cars aren't just typical software developers who write programs for desktop computers, laptop computers, or handheld mobile devices. People who write programs for automobiles or other nontraditional computer devices with specific hardware concerns are known as embedded software developers. Embedded software developers must consider the hardware they are working with—its capabilities, limitations, and intended functions—to make the device, a car in this case, work properly.

The Fiat Chrysler Ram 1500 is not your traditional pickup truck. It boasts a convenient computer touchscreen for controlling cabin functions.

To become a successful automobile-focused embedded software developer, an aspiring candidate needs to not only be an expert code writer but also must understand cars inside and out. "Many software developers who get into an automotive job feel really lost regarding the kind of software they find there. It is so different compared to other kinds of software like web, desktop and even mobile applications," wrote embedded software engineer Viktor Schepik in a blog post.

For instance, a software program might control the steering of a car, so the steering wheel and tires aren't actually connected by anything but a wire that carries input from one to the other. Nissan actually brought a steer "by wire" system to the market as early as 2013. While other systems went electronic much earlier, steering is a little more complicated because it can be frightening to envision front wheels that don't respond to a driver's input but are instead entirely dependent on a computer's judgment.

Nissan worked around this problem by including a fail-safe clutch in the steering column so if one of the three control modules overseeing the electric steering detects a fault, the clutch can snap shut and act as a traditional rack-and-pinion system. This backup also allows the driver to steer the car while pushing if the car fails to start. But if all goes according to plan, the only things telling the wheels what to do are the computer control modules. They report the driver's desired steering angle instantaneously to the motors that turn the car's wheels. This allows the car to move as the driver directs it, just like in a traditional steering setup. However, electric steering insulates the driver from road impacts. For example, if the car hits a pothole, the steering wheel won't jerk in response. Because steering input will remain accurate even if the car is, for example, sliding on a slippery road, electric steering may potentially increase safety. When designing this system, an embedded software engineer had to take all of these considerations into account.

So what's the difference between a regular software engineer and an embedded software engineer? Knowledge of hardware, for one. Because software developers for desktop computers and mobile apps are typically shielded from the hardware the applications will eventually run on, they don't necessarily have to know much about the hardware. For embedded software developers, however, the entire point of their labor is to make the hardware function correctly as it is intended to. Without a thorough knowledge of the hardware, an embedded software engineer can't write code that will control or use the hardware in the best possible way. Knowledge of hardware is essential to create software that will exploit its capabilities to best effect.

LEARNING THE RULES OF CODE

MISRA C is a comprehensive set of coding rules for the C and C++ programming languages laid out by the Motor Industry Software Reliability Association. These rules serve to define a safer subset of the language suitable for any type of development project. MISRA C coding guidelines set the international benchmark for all software written in C and C++. MISRA C is used not only in the development of passenger cars but in the aerospace, telecom, medical, defense, and railway industries.

The MISRA C guidelines were first established in 1998, shortly after the United States required every vehicle produced or sold in the country to adopt computers for OBD. The 127 rules of MISRA C: 1998 were updated to include 142 rules in 2004, 143 rules in 2012, and 14 new security guidelines in 2016. Mandatory compliance to MISRA C rules ensure that embedded software engineers hew to safe standards when coding new functionalities in automobiles that will eventually carry passengers.

C STUDENTS

The C programming language is used for embedded software programming, such as programming the computer elements of cars. C programming language is the base of embedded software programming. Experts in the field recommend becoming so well versed in C that you think in the language.

Some programmers consider C a more difficult language to learn than others, but programmer Evan Miller compares it to learning to drive a stick shift, maintaining that knowledge of its structure ultimately makes students better at programming in any language. "C forces you to build a mental model of what the computer is actually doing when you run your programs," Miller wrote in a blog post quoted on the website Lifehacker.

Using that mental model to encompass the process, CPU architecture, memory hierarchy, and operating system will follow naturally as you continue to ask questions and search for answers. Ultimately, this will help simplify abstractions and enable you to write truly innovative programs.

If you want to get a jump on learning C before going to college, there are numerous online tutorials and books available on the basics of the language. Websites such as Learn-C.org, which offers a free interactive tutorial that doesn't require any downloads, offer introductory challenges to help verse yourself in the language. To hone your skills

Becoming fluent in C provides a boost for any aspiring embedded software engineer. C is the language of computer-enabled objects.

sufficiently to become an embedded software engineer, Maharajan Veerabahu, co-founder of e-con Systems, an embedded product development services company, recommends attempting to write at least one C program every day. This level of familiarity with the language is necessary when it comes to applying it to complicated hardware.

CAR HACKING

In 2015, cybersecurity researchers Charlie Miller and Chris Valasek undertook an experiment for *Wired* magazine in which they remotely hacked a Jeep being driven by *Wired* writer Andy Greenberg. Though Greenberg never touched the dashboard, cold air started blasting from the vents at maximum setting. Next, the radio began blaring music at full volume, despite Greenberg's efforts to turn it down. The windshield wipers turned on, and wiper fluid shot up to blur the glass.

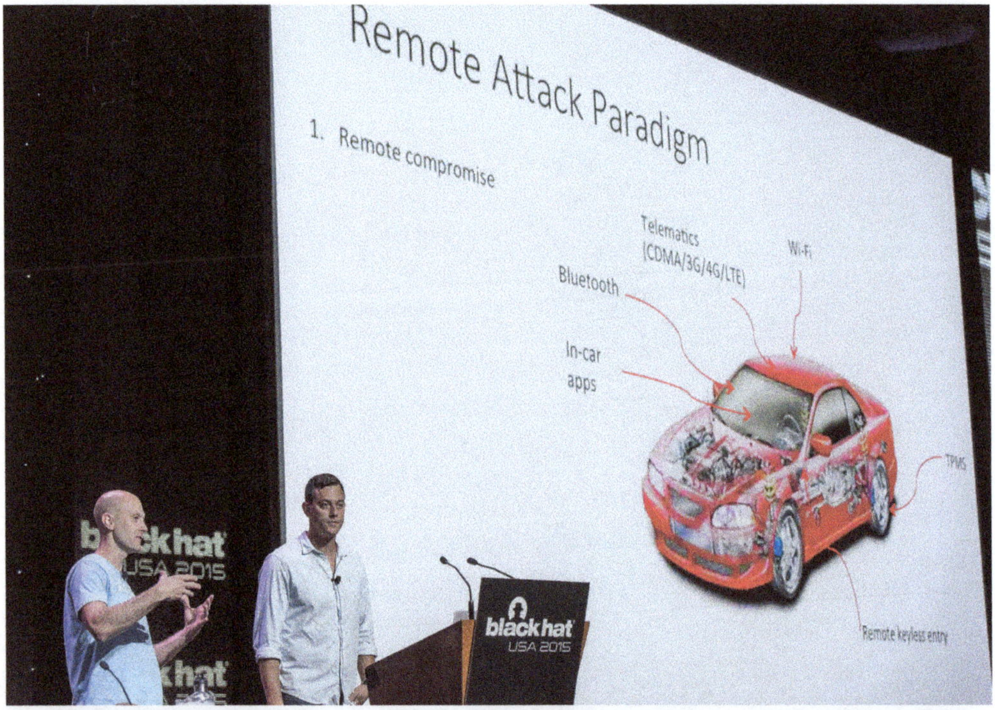

Cybersecurity experts Charlie Miller (*left*) and Chris Valasek speak at a developer conference about their experiment remotely hacking a Jeep.

Eventually, from the comfort of a couch approximately 10 miles (16 km) away, the two hackers cut power to the accelerator, leaving Greenberg motionless and stranded on Interstate 64 until he called and asked them to stop. From a safer empty parking lot, the hackers demonstrated even more disturbing power over the vehicle, ultimately cutting the brakes and sending Greenberg rolling uncontrollably into a ditch.

Following publication of the article Greenberg wrote describing the experience, Fiat Chrysler recalled 1.4 million Jeep, Ram, Dodge, and Chrysler vehicles that contained the same Uconnect infotainment system Miller and Valasek exploited to leave Greenberg stranded on the interstate. In fact, Chrysler actually sent owners of the affected vehicles USB sticks they could plug into the cars to perform the necessary update themselves!

Today, Miller and Valasek work as cybersecurity experts for Cruise Automation, a GM subsidiary that focuses on the development of computer-driven cars. In an interview with *Car and Driver* magazine, Miller stated that he is confident that cars of the future can be made safe from potential hacking attacks: "We just need to systematically apply what we know, take our time, and do it right."

Securing a car is easier in some ways than securing a network of computers, according to Miller. "It's still a lot of computers, but they're used in predictable ways and we have a lot of control over the environment," he explained. For instance, a car is more securable than a network of laptops that people

This computer-driven Chevrolet Bolt was built by Cruise Automation, a company for which Charlie Miller and Chris Valasek work as cybersecurity experts.

carry around to various locations and use to surf the web. The computers in a car are only going to be used to perform a regular pattern of actions for driving to and fro.

Miller's job is made easier by the fact that he is working to secure computer-automated cars for a ride-sharing firm, where cars will return to the company to receive maintenance. It will be harder for companies that manufacture cars to secure their vehicles effectively, Miller pointed out, since once they are released to the customer, it's more difficult to implement updates. Nobody will ever be able to make any computer system completely unhackable, Miller asserted, but it's possible to make hacking a car so difficult that no one will feasibly be able to undertake the task.

Hacking cars is a difficult undertaking, Miller admitted. Ultimately, the task of securing personal automobiles will require that automakers and suppliers follow established safety protocols, perform necessary checks and tests, and secure third-party validation.

CHAPTER FOUR

DIGITAL AUTO MECHANICS

It's clear that modern cars aren't merely mechanical assemblages. Instead, they run on complex computers that constantly measure, communicate, and make adjustments to the engine, drivetrain, and suspension. A single car contains as many as fifty ECUs to control functions like acceleration and braking. When you buy a car, you purchase this functionality, but you don't own the proprietary software in its computers. Though the software is copyrighted and belongs to the manufacturers, it is possible to rewrite code to make the ECUs behave as you please, to make the car faster, more fuel efficient, or more powerful.

"FLASHING" AND THE FUTURE

Modders, or people who make aftermarket changes to a vehicle, such as the creators of RomRaider and OpenECU, have built open source software to make changes to their cars' ECUs. CanBusHack, Inc., is "a

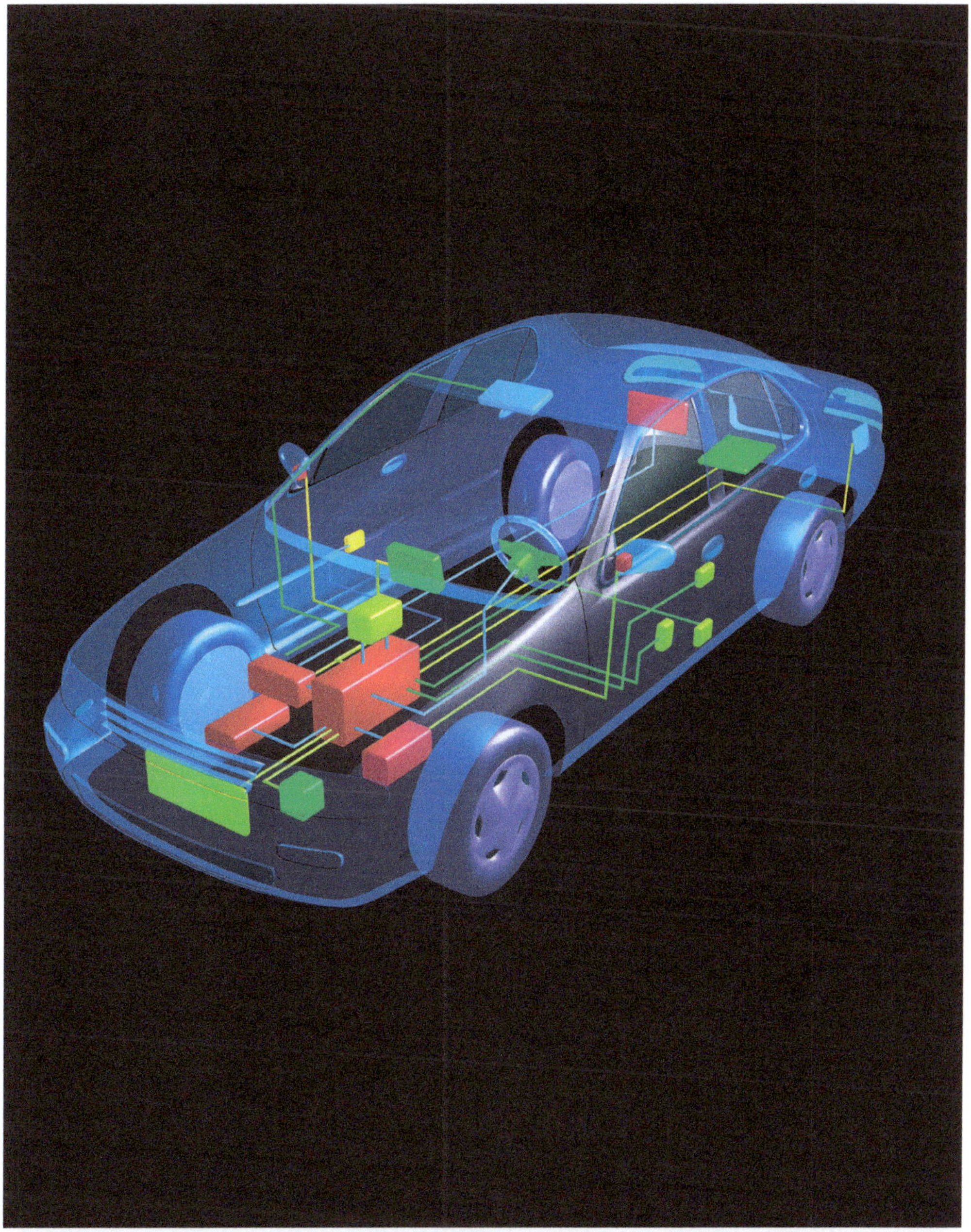

Modern cars are made up of complex networks of computers and wires. This requires auto mechanics to be computer specialists so that they can target and fix problems.

reverse engineering services corporation specializing in automotive embedded controller software and communication understanding," according to the group's website. That's a long way from the then relatively new "flash programming" Dan Maslic described in an article for *Underhood Service* in 2004.

"Flashing," as Maslic wrote, refers to reprogramming a car's ECUs after production. "Going back to the basics," Maslic explained, "you know that all automotive engine and powertrain control modules (PCMs) are essentially small-sized, dedicated computers. They have a microprocessor, built-in random access memory (RAM), signal-conditioning chips (for sensor inputs), output transistor/drivers (for actuating ignition coils and fuel injectors) and a programmable read-only memory-type chip (PROM) for calibration purposes."

The PROM is the important part when it comes to flash reprogramming since it contains the calibration information for the ECU. When the car's ignition turns and the ECU boots up like a tiny computer, one of its tasks is reading the PROM, which calibrates the ECU so it knows how much fuel it should inject, how much spark advance is required, and so on. Therefore, changing the PROM can change how the ECU computer controls the engine.

Older PROMs, however, were able to be programmed only once. If a PROM was programmed with a certain calibration, it couldn't be changed; if a mechanic wanted to add an update, he or she would have to buy a whole new PROM and install it. But advances quickly brought about erasable, reprogrammable PROMs—EPROMs and EEPROMs.

THE IMPORTANCE OF SHOP

Whether you want to work to fix cars, design them, or familiarize yourself with their workings, you should take an automotive shop class. In 2014, Evan Fischbach, then only two years out of high school, was already earning $40,000 per year as a technician for LaFontaine Chrysler-Dodge-Jeep-Ram, according to an article in *Automotive News*. Fischbach was propelled directly into the workforce after taking an automotive shop class during his junior year of high school in Saline, Michigan, when a local dealership hired him to work as an apprentice in the service bay. Straight out of high school, he began earning approximately three times more than the average for a nineteen-year-old high school graduate, slightly more than the national median.

If you want to work as an auto technician, shop class can potentially qualify you for a job directly after high school. Businesses that need automotive workers may find themselves competing to recruit qualified candidates straight out of high school.

Learning about the mechanical aspect of automobiles is also necessary for those who wish to work in programming cars' inner computers. "It's a great pity that it is so hard to get into the automobile way of thinking of how to build embedded software," wrote embedded software engineer Viktor Schepik in a blog post about breaking into the industry.

(continued on the next page)

(continued from the previous page)

Familiarization with both the C programming language and the basic functions and purposes of various mechanical aspects of automobiles can go a long way toward adequately preparing an aspiring embedded software engineer for the tasks of the job. "As for wired kids preparing for wired jobs in a wired world, even the most sophisticated design software can't substitute for an appreciation of how materials truly behave in a finished product. The choices an engineer or designer makes while creating a new product are often determined by what happens during the fabrication process," wrote Joe Astroth in an article for the Huffington Post. Without a solid understanding of the device being programmed, an embedded software engineer can't hope to successfully take advantage of its capabilities and make it function properly.

THE SPEED OF TECHNOLOGY

By the early 1990s, technicians were able to erase and reprogram EEPROMs merely by hooking a scan tool up to the vehicle. This process was much easier than removing the ECU, removing the PROM, obtaining the part ID number, ordering a new PROM, and then reinstalling everything.

Flash-PROMs allow the entire programming to be erased and reprogrammed in one continuous step, eliminating potential sources of error in the process.

An ECU isolated from a car might not look like much, but in reality it's one of the "brains" of the modern vehicle.

Previously, auto shops didn't carry stock to replace PROMs. It just wasn't practical, as Maslic's example proves: a single 1990 Chevrolet Lumina has at least twenty-eight different PROMs. Technicians were forced to special order a PROM if they wanted to take care of a specific technical service bulletin (a manufacturer-recommended procedure for repairing a vehicle) for that car.

By 2004, the speed of technology had changed everything. With the advent of OBD II, the size of vehicle calibration files increased and, along with it, the potential for complication. These days, addressing software issues is a common part of a mechanic's job. So what does this mean in practice?

A typical flash programming system consists of a personal computer, an automotive scan tool, an off-board programming power supply, a cable/harness set, and the calibration software itself. In 2004, Maslic estimated that charges for flash reprogramming were approximately $80 to $120 for what amounted to about thirty to fifty minutes of work: bringing the car into the bay, establishing a connection with the scan tool, reading the calibration, performing the reprogramming, and returning the car to the lot. Progress and the application of new technology change the industry and force mechanics to do business in different ways and provide new services to customers. By 2018, flash programming was no longer a novelty but a routine part of any competent technician's work.

CHAPTER FIVE

DRIVING INTO THE FUTURE

Car coders not only have to think about how to write the most effective algorithms to make the machinery respond in the intended fashion, they also must consider human psychology at the same time. This consideration comes into sharp focus with the future of driverless cars. In terms of saving lives, driverless vehicles should make sense. Removing the possibility of driver fatigue or alcohol impairment could potentially reduce the fatality rate in the United States by 45.5 percent. However, some things that make sense on paper don't translate accurately to real life. In 2018, in Tempe, Arizona, a woman was struck and killed by a self-driving Uber vehicle.

The human brain assesses risk very differently. Even though computer-controlled cars should be safer than human drivers, it is more difficult for the average person to place trust in a machine than in another human driver. In 2016, then-head of the National Highway Traffic Safety Administration (NHTSA) Mark

The outer design of this Tesla driverless truck reflects the futuristic technology hard at work under the vehicle's hood.

Rosekind estimated that a driverless fleet would have to increase safety at least twofold to gain government approval. This would mean cutting the current toll of approximately 40,200 vehicular deaths per year to less than 20,100, and even that might not be enough to convince individual drivers to place their safety in the "hands" of computers.

Research shows that people tend to feel less safe riding as a passenger in a car than they do when they are personally driving, perceiving a greater sense of control over the vehicle. When a person is behind the wheel, he or she also tends to suffer less carsickness than that person would while riding in the passenger seat, where one does not feel a sense of control over the vehicle.

The perception of personal control over the vehicle tends to make people feel less risk averse, while riding as a passenger makes risk feel more involuntary and thus frightening. "The rational utilitarian view is that we should trust the machines versus us as long as they're even the slightest bit better," said Gill Pratt, CEO of Toyota Research Institute. "Our hypothesis is that, because it's hard to empathize with a machine compared with a person, society is going to hold machines to a higher standard." That also means that embedded software developers who create the programs for autonomously driven vehicles will be held to a higher standard. Not only is designing automotive software programs an exciting job on the constant cusp of innovation, it also demands perfection because passengers' safety is at stake.

MODELING CARS INTO EXISTENCE

Computers have also revolutionized car building in different ways. Computer modeling allows car manufacturers to produce vehicles more efficiently than ever before, reducing testing times and allowing engineers to play with ideas more easily.

Ford is analyzing miles per gallon with computer modeling, Chrysler is using state-of-the-art modeling to

3D rendering allows for extremely accurate wind testing, for example, without having to physically place the car within a wind tunnel.

design better factories, and Mercedes-Benz uses computer modeling to test solutions for better aerodynamics. At Chrysler, computers track inventory and perform 3D modeling to simulate safety, installation, and risk analysis for power train and engine assembly. This modeling is used to train factory workers how best and most efficiently to assemble the vehicle, combining computer efficiency with human expertise to maximize productivity.

However, this doesn't mean Chrysler wants to or even can replace human workers with computational analysis. "There is an intellectual property you get with humans that you don't get with robots," Chrysler vice president in charge of power train manufacturing Brian Harlow told TechRadar. "Robots only do what you program them to do. A human worker can avoid damage to expensive parts and give feedback about the safety handling and ergonomics involved with the installation." In 2014, Mercedes-Benz used virtual aerodynamic testing to perfect its CLA sedan. Using computational fluid dynamics, Mercedes-Benz developers are able to model and better understand the airflow around and through the vehicle while it is in motion.

The computer program used to map airflow generates what Patrick Höfer, leader of the Mercedes-Benz aerodynamics compact cars team, called "flow visualisation pictures," which allow the design team to find potential problems in the vehicle's aerodynamics. Using computer modeling, engineers can assess the car's streamlines and analyze factors such as pressure distribution and wake structure. The computer-visualized airflow around the front wheels influenced design decisions for the car's structure. The computerized aerodynamic testing offered Mercedes-Benz much more data than would be available in a traditional physical wind tunnel test. With this level of precision, designers are able to directly correlate a drag coefficient value to mileage, offering an unprecedented amount of control over the resultant vehicle's gas mileage.

Computer modeling to determine miles per gallon has also improved in recent years. In the past, separate models would have determined data for the combustion system, transmission, battery, and even climate control settings and aerodynamics. Now these separate models are correlated to calculate the miles-per-gallon rating. Computerized modeling allows Ford, for example, to predict the experience of the average user at various speeds. For an electrically powered plug-in vehicle, computer modeling can predict rates of charge and efficiency for a driver who charges at stations during the day rather than overnight.

Modeling can also offer insight into the effect of the warm-up processes of a car: for a driver who makes a single trip to work and then comes home at night or for a driver who makes several short trips throughout the day. "All energy used comes from the fuel or from the power utility," Mazen Hammoud, the chief engineer of power train electrification at Ford, told TechRadar. "This even includes using the heated seats or adjusting the seats. We try to re-generate energy, but to start with, all energy comes from these two sources. All energy you use can reduce mileage." And all energy sources and potential drains can be modeled effectively using computer technology. Ultimately, the models will assess all values inside the car and generate a single number to define the car's energy usage. For now, the data is used to create an average predicated on real-world testing to verify lab findings.

CLOUD-BASED BUILDING ASSISTANCE

Cloud-based tooling data is rapidly on the rise. The MachiningCloud app is essentially a data aggregator that provides carmakers with data from cutting tool suppliers and simulation software products. This technology isn't just a digital tool catalog; it contains process knowledge that can speed up production times. This saves automotive technicians hours of labor spent researching parts and cross-referencing catalogs to find what they need. With this data, contributing editor Ray Chalmers in an article for

Kennametal's NOVO is a cloud-based tooling application that lets mechanics easily access the precise information they need.

Automotive Design & Production, explained, automotive workers can access setup advice and application-specific instructions with just a few clicks of a button.

This allows car builders to easily access the precise knowledge they need to proceed. For example, rather than wondering which specific tool would be

COMPUTERIZED "GUTS"

When most people think of car design, they think of the exterior of the vehicle, the sheet metal. The vice president of Nissan Design America, Taro Ueda, has a different view of vehicle design, one suited to a generation of young people who are more interested in the capabilities of their cell phones than the look of their car. Ueda himself doesn't believe that exterior vehicle design is necessarily less important than it was before the digital era but stated that consumers need more value for the vehicle.

Ueda believes car design should holistically consider every aspect of the car user's experience, integrating technology to facilitate a smooth and pleasant driving experience. "There is a physical and digital interaction that occurs during the sequence of simply getting into the vehicle," he told *Automotive Design & Production*. "Perhaps we can design the entire experience so that it is a little bit better."

most appropriate for a task, a designer can use Kennametal's NOVO application to search the cloud by typing in the specifications for the task they need to accomplish and almost immediately receive the best recommendation and related information. "Hours turn into minutes and users get the assurance that the list is both comprehensive, correct and up to date," Chalmers wrote. "All of this leads to less misapplication of tooling, more optimal machining strategies, and increased productivity with better production quality."

DATA AND DRIVING HABITS

The era of Big Data has arrived for the automobile. Companies such as Mercedes-Benz and Ford use computer learning to cater to driver's individual preferences. Mercedes-Benz's tracking system takes note of what time the car is usually driven, keeps track of what radio stations are preferred at various times of day, and can monitor real-time traffic problems on preferred routes to save a driver time. The car is now capable of making such intelligent decisions that it almost seems to be becoming aware.

Ford's tracking system for hybrid cars measures drivers' daily routes to maximize fuel economy. The data generated by the tracking program can alter how the car behaves, making it switch to gasoline to generate power for a long drive or switch over to electric power when the car is close to home and presumably will soon be able to recharge. And this doesn't require the driver to punch in a destination on GPS. Because the car has learned the driver's usual routines, it will automatically know to take its passenger to work in the morning, for example.

Even the sensitivity with which a driver places his or her foot on the accelerator and brakes is monitored by tracking systems. A "black box" stores a record of activity in the last few seconds before a crash, for instance, so law enforcement and insurers can

A black box recorder allows investigators to determine precisely what was happening in the vehicle's systems at the time of a crash.

determine whether driver performance played a factor in the accident.

As computer capabilities in cars continue to improve, motor vehicles will be able to communicate with one another, sharing information about traffic, weather, and road conditions, even broadcasting their speed and potential road hazards to other nearby vehicles. This vehicle-to-vehicle communication, called V2V for short, is already in testing stages. A pilot program by the University of Michigan and the US Department of Transportation saw three thousand

V2V-equipped vehicles turned loose to drive around the streets of Ann Arbor, Michigan, and gather information about the effectiveness of the technology.

The V2V-equipped cars and trucks emit a short-range signal ten times per second that can be detected by other vehicles, helping determine whether a potential accident is imminent. Cars equipped with the devices also beep warnings when they are about to encounter obstacles or are going too fast in unsafe conditions.

In 2014, federal officials estimated that V2V technology could help prevent up to 76 percent of crashes on US roads. In fact, the NHTSA intends to require V2V technology on future cars and light trucks.

V2V crash-avoidance technology has the potential to greatly increase safety and reduce the number of crashes on US roadways, according to NHTSA acting administrator David Friedman. He told CNN, "Decades from now, it's likely we'll look back at this time period as one in which the historical arc of transportation safety considerably changed for the better."

GLOSSARY

automotive technician A mechanic who can service a wide variety of vehicles.

C A general-purpose computer programming language, commonly used in embedded software development.

CANbus Controller area network, a vehicle bus standard designed to allow microcontrollers and devices to communicate with each other in applications without a host computer.

cloud An information technology paradigm that allows access to a shared pool of data.

code Instructions for a computer program.

computer An electronic device for storing and processing data.

computer modeling A computer program designed to emulate what might happen in a particular situation.

deep learning A machine learning method based on data representations rather than task-specific algorithms.

electronic control unit (ECU) An embedded system that controls one or more of the electrical systems in an automobile.

embedded software engineer A developer who designs code for a machine or device not typically thought of as a computer.

emissions control The study and practice of reducing motor vehicle emissions, which are harmful to the environment.

hardware The physical parts that make up a computer system.

On-Board Diagnostics (OBD) The system that allows vehicles to self-diagnose and report problems.

machine code A computer programming language consisting of binary or hexadecimal instructions that a computer can respond to directly.

MISRA C The set of software development guidelines for the C programming language developed by the Motor Industry Software Reliability Association.

modder Someone who makes aftermarket changes to a vehicle.

program A collection of instructions that performs a specific task when executed by a computer.

programming language A language used to write instructions for a computer; the instructions may then be translated into machine code.

programmable read-only memory (PROM) A type of chip used to calibrate ECUs so they are configured to run in a particular engine.

software The part of a computer system that consists of data or computer instructions.

software developer A person who uses programming language to write instructions for a computer to carry out.

V2V Vehicle-to-vehicle communication.

FOR MORE INFORMATION

Automotive News Canada
PO Box 243, Station A
Windsor, ON N9A 6K7
Canada
(877) 812-1257
Website: http://canada.autonews.com
A good source of up-to-date data on the automotive industry in Canada.

Automotive Service Association
8209 Mid Cities Blvd.
North Richland Hills, TX 76182-4712
(817) 514-2900
Website: http://asashop.org
This organization advances professionalism and excellence in the automotive repair industry through education, representation, and member services.

Embedded
Aspencore Inc.
1225 Franklin Ave., Suite 400
Garden City, NY 11530
(256) 319-0257
Website: https://www.embedded.com
A resource for embedded systems designers and developers.

Institute of Electrical and Electronics Engineers
3 Park Avenue, 17th Floor
New York, NY 10016-5997

(800) 678-4333
Website: https://www.ieee.org
The world's largest organization of technical professionals.

National Institute for Automotive Service Excellence
1503 Edwards Ferry Road NE, Suite 401
Leesburg, VA 20176
(703) 669-6600
Website: http://www.ase.com
An independent certifying body for automotive professionals.

USCAR
1000 Town Center Drive, Suite 300
Southfield, MI 48075
(248) 223-9000
Website: http://www.uscar.org
USCAR creates, supports, and directs US cooperative research and development to advance automotive technologies.

FOR FURTHER READING

Grenning, James. *Test-Driven Development for Embedded C* (Pragmatic Programmers). Dallas, TX: Pragmatic Bookshelf, 2011.

Halderman, James. *Automotive Technology: Principles, Diagnosis, and Service*. Seattle, WA: Pearson, 2015.

Heitmann, John. *The Automobile and American Life*. Jefferson, NC: McFarland & Company, 2009.

Hobbs, Chris. *Embedded Software Development for Safety-Critical Systems*. Boca Raton, FL: Auerbach Publications, 2015.

Kochan, Stephen. *Programming in C*. Upper Saddle River, NJ: Addison-Wesley Professional, 2014.

Lipson, Hod, and Melba Kurman. *Driverless: Intelligent Cars and the Road Ahead*. Cambridge, MA: MIT Press, 2017.

Liu, Shaoshan, Liyun Li, and Jie Tang. *Creating Autonomous Vehicle Systems* (Synthesis Lectures on Computer Science). San Rafael, CA: Morgan & Claypool Publishers, 2017.

Martin, Tracy. *How to Use Automotive Diagnostic Scanners*. Minneapolis, MN: Motorbooks, 2015.

Parissien, Steven. *The Life of the Automobile: The Complete History of the Motor Car*. New York, NY: Thomas Dunne Books, 2014.

Perry, Greg, and Dean Miller. *C Programming Absolute Beginner's Guide*. Seattle, WA: Que Publishing, 2013.

BIBLIOGRAPHY

Astroth, Joe. "Why Shop Class Is Still Relevant." Huffington Post, May 19, 2011. https://www.huffingtonpost.com/joe-astroth/why-shop-class-relevant_b_862801.html.

Atiyeh, Clifford. "Fiat Chrysler Recalls 1.4 Million Cars to Prevent Hacking." *Car and Driver*, July 24, 2015. https://blog.caranddriver.com/fiat-chrysler-recalls-1-4-million-cars-to-prevent-hacking.

Bach, Jonathan, and Mike Colias. "Is It a Car or a Computer?" *Wall Street Journal*, September 13, 2016. https://www.wsj.com/articles/is-it-a-car-or-a-computer-1474251122.

Barreto, Victor, and Daniella Mooers. "What Is OBD II? History of On-Board Diagnostics." Geotab, August 18, 2017. https://www.geotab.com/blog/obd-ii.

Beard, David. "This Is the Tech Fully Autonomous (Level 5) Cars Will Need to Have." *Car and Driver,* October 2017. https://www.caranddriver.com/features/this-is-the-tech-fully-autonomous-level-5-cars-will-need-to-have-feature.

Berg, Phil. "10 Diagnostic Apps and Devices to Make You a Better Driver." *Popular Mechanics*, February 21, 2012. https://www.popularmechanics.com/cars/how-to/g767/10-diagnostic-apps-and-devices-to-make-you-a-better-driver.

Brandon, John. "How Computers Have Revolutionized Our Cars." TechRadar, July 4, 2013. https://www.techradar.com/news/car-tech/how-computers-have-revolutionised-car-design-1160141.

CAN in Automation. "History of CAN Technology." Retrieved March 2, 2018. https://www.can-cia.org/can-knowledge/can/can-history.

Chalmers, Ray. "Speeding Production with Digital Tooling." *Automotive Design & Production*, January 24, 2018. https://www.adandp.media/articles/speeding-production-with-digital-tooling.

Colwell, K. C. "Electric Feel: Nissan Digitizes Steering, but the Wheel Remains." *Car and Driver*, January 2013. https://www.caranddriver.com/features/electric-feel-nissan-digitizes-steering-but-the-wheel-remains-feature.

Crow, Dan. "Why Every Child Should Learn to Code." *Guardian* (Manchester), February 7, 2014. https://www.theguardian.com/technology/2014/feb/07/year-of-code-dan-crow-songkick.

Curtis, Sophie. "The Car of the Future Is 'The Most Powerful Computer You Will Ever Own.'" *Telegraph* (London), May 17, 2015. https://www.telegraph.co.uk/technology/news/11609406/The-car-of-the-future-is-the-most-powerful-computer-you-will-ever-own.html.

Gall, Jared. "Can a Connected Car Ever Be Safe from Hacking?" *Car and Driver*, October 2017. https://www.caranddriver.com/features/can-a-connected-car-ever-be-safe-from-hacking-feature.

Greenberg, Andy. "Hackers Remotely Kill a Jeep on the Highway—with Me in It." *Wired*, July 21, 2015. https://www.wired.com/2015/07/hackers-remotely-kill-jeep-highway.

Griggs, Brandon. "Cars That Talk to Each Other." CNN. Retrieved March 2, 2018. http://www.cnn.com/interactive/2014/02/tech/cnn10-future-of-driving.

IEEE Spectrum. February 1, 2009. Retrieved April 27, 2018. https://spectrum.ieee.org/transportation/systems/this-car-runs-on-code.

Kurczewski, Nick. "We Drive 'Deep-Learning' Audi at CES 2017." Cars.com, January 6, 2017. https://www.cars.com/articles/we-drive-deep-learning-audi-at-ces-2017-1420692904466.

Maslic, Dan. "Flash! Reprogramming Vehicle Computers." *Underhood Service*, December 1, 2004. http://www.underhoodservice.com/flash-reprogramming-vehicle-computers.

Mertl, Steve. "How Cars Have Become Rolling Computers." *Toronto Globe and Mail*, March 5, 2016. https://www.theglobeandmail.com/globe-drive/how-cars-have-become-rolling-computers/article29008154.

Motavalli, Jim. "The Dozens of Computers That Make Modern Cars Go (and Stop)." *New York Times*, February 4, 2010. http://www.nytimes.com/2010/02/05/technology/05electronics.html.

Motor Industry Software Reliability Association. "What Is MISRA?" Retrieved March 2, 2018. https://www.misra.org.uk.

Schepik, Viktor. "How to Be an Automobile Software Engineer." Medium, October 20, 2015. https://medium.com/@viktorschepik/how-to-be-an-automobile-software-engineer-part-1

-7729a780d89b.

Stoklosa, Alexander. “Up to 472 HP: Ford Performance Unveils Power Packs for 2015–2017 Mustang GT.” *Car and Driver*, July 28, 2016. https://blog.caranddriver.com/up-to-472-hp-ford-performance-unveils-power-packs-for-2015-2017-mustang-gt.

Valdes-Dapena, Peter. “Cars That Collect Data About You.” CNNMoney. Retrieved March 2, 2018. http://www.cnn.com/interactive/2014/02/tech/cnn10-future-of-driving.

Vasilash, Gary. “Taro Ueda and Designing for Today.” *Automotive Design & Production*, January 25, 2018. https://www.adandp.media/articles/taro-ueda-and-designing-for-today.

Veerabahu, Maharajan. “5 Differences Between Embedded Software Engineer and Software Developer.” LinkedIn, December 19, 2014. https://www.linkedin.com/pulse/5-differences-between-embedded-maharajan.

Wiens, Kyle. “WTF! It Should Not Be Illegal to Hack Your Own Car’s Computer.” *Wired*, January 23, 2015. https://www.wired.com/2015/01/let-us-hack-our-cars.

Wojdyla, Ben. “How It Works: The Computer Inside Your Car.” *Popular Mechanics*, February 21, 2012. https://www.popularmechanics.com/cars/how-to/a7386/how-it-works-the-computer-inside-your-car.

INDEX

E

F

G

H

I

K

L

M

N

O

P

R

S

ABOUT THE AUTHOR

Jennifer Culp is an author of nonfiction science and technology books for young adults.

PHOTO CREDITS

Cover REB Images/Blend Images/Getty Images; back cover and pp. 4–5 (background) nadla/E+/Getty Images; p. 5 © iStockphoto.com/Sjoerd van der Wal; pp. 7, 22, 37, 48, 55 AMatveev/Shutterstock.com ; p. 9 Ahsanriaz6157 /Wikimedia Commons/File: CANbus and ECU.JPG/CC BY-SA 4.0; pp. 12–13 Vchal/Shutterstock.com; pp. 16–17 VanderWolf Images/Shutterstock.com; p. 20 Hadrian /Shutterstock.com; p. 23 Wavebreakmedia/iStock /Thinkstock; pp. 24–25 © iStockphoto.com/BanksPhotos; p. 28 Kim Kulish/Corbis News/Getty Images; pp. 32–33, 38–39, 44 Bloomberg/Getty Images; p. 35 Adventtr/E+ /Getty Images; p. 43 Valentin Wolf/Getty Images; p. 46 Dllu/Wikimedia Commons/File:Cruise Automation Bolt EV third generation in San Francisco.jpg/CC BY-SA 4.0; p. 49 Alfred Pasieka/Science Photo Library/Getty Images; p. 53 Petar Jankovic/Alamy Stock Photo; p. 56 Reuters Staff /REUTERS/Newscom; pp. 58–59 VRX/Shutterstock.com; p. 62 Casimiro/Alamy Stock Photo; p. 65 Pool/Getty Images; interior design graphic (abstract circuit) Titima Ongkantong/Shutterstock.com.

Design: Michael Moy; Layout: Nicole Russo-Duca; Photo Researcher: Sherri Jackson